THE EVOLUTION OF
Amphibians

by Andrea Pelleschi

Content Consultant

David C. Blackburn
Associate Curator of Amphibians and Reptiles
Florida Museum of Natural History

Essential Library
An Imprint of Abdo Publishing | abdobooks.com

ANIMAL EVOLUTION

abdobooks.com

Published by Abdo Publishing, a division of ABDO, PO Box 398166, Minneapolis, Minnesota 55439. Copyright © 2019 by Abdo Consulting Group, Inc. International copyrights reserved in all countries. No part of this book may be reproduced in any form without written permission from the publisher. Essential Library™ is a trademark and logo of Abdo Publishing.

Printed in the United States of America, North Mankato, Minnesota.
092018
012019

THIS BOOK CONTAINS
RECYCLED MATERIALS

Cover Photo: Shutterstock Images
Interior Photos: De Agostini Picture Library/Science Source, 4; New York Public Library/Science Source, 6; Shutterstock Images, 8, 9, 27, 39, 41, 51, 52, 54–55; Rudmer Zwerver/Shutterstock Images, 10; Everett Historical/Shutterstock, 13; iStockphoto, 14, 49; Galina Savina/Shutterstock Images, 16–17; Faviel Raven/Shutterstock Images, 19; The Natural History Museum, London/Science Source, 24; Joy Lee/The Philadelphia Inquirer/AP Images, 25; Phil Degginger/Geological Enterprises/Science Source, 28–29; Phil Degginger/Carnegie Museum/Science Source, 30; Red Line Editorial, 31; Walter Myers/Science Source, 35; Dorling Kindersley/Science Source, 42–43; Paul D. Stewart/Science Source, 45; Stephen Roberts/De Agostini Picture Library/Universal Images Group/Newscom, 46; Paulo de Oliveira/NHPA/Avalon/Newscom, 56; Dan Suzio/Science Source, 58; Michel Gunther/Science Source, 61; Francis Bossé/Shutterstock Images, 63; Bruno Cavignaux/Science Source, 66–67; Tristan Tan/Shutterstock Images, 69; Dante Fenolio/Science Source, 70, 80–81, 83, 86; Chris Mattison/FLPA/Science Source, 71; Suzanne L. & Joseph T. Collins/Science Source, 72; Jay Ondreicka/Shutterstock Images, 73; Chris Mattison/agefotostock/Newscom, 74; Dirk Ercken/Shutterstock Images, 75; ER Degginger/Science Source, 76, 79; Nick Pike/De Agostini Picture Library/Universal Images Group/Newscom, 85; Pete Oxford/Minden Pictures/Newscom, 87; Dan Sykes/Natural History Museum, London/Science Source, 90; Philippe Psaila/Science Source, 93, 97; Jose Luis Calvo/Shutterstock Images, 95; Kurit Afshen/Shutterstock Images, 98; Arnulfo Franco/AP Images, 99

Editor: Marie Pearson
Series Designer: Becky Daum

Library of Congress Control Number: 2018947965

Publisher's Cataloging-in-Publication Data

Names: Pelleschi, Andrea, author.
Title: The evolution of amphibians / by Andrea Pelleschi.
Description: Minneapolis, Minnesota : Abdo Publishing, 2019 | Series: Animal evolution | Includes online resources and index.
Identifiers: ISBN 9781532116629 (lib. bdg.) | ISBN 9781532159466 (ebook)
Subjects: LCSH: Amphibians--Evolution--Juvenile literature. | Animal evolution--Juvenile literature. | Biological evolution--Juvenile literature. | Amphibians--Juvenile literature.
Classification: DDC 574.30--dc23

CONTENTS

CHAPTER ONE

Out of the Water

Approximately 360 million years ago (MYA), in what is now Greenland, a brawny animal about three feet (1 m) long swam in a river.[1] *Ichthyostega* looked like a short alligator or a large iguana, but it had a thick neck and a wide head. Using its four squat limbs and tail, it propelled itself through the currents, eating small fish and breathing with its gills. Sometimes it walked along the bottom of the river, and sometimes it left the river entirely and stepped onto land.

How did it do this? Why did it leave the water? Perhaps there was a long rainy period, and the animal found itself in the shallow waters of a floodplain. Maybe it just wandered onto dry land.

An artist depicts what *Ichthyostega* may have looked like.

During the Devonian period, Earth was warm and wet.

When the animal was in shallow water, it used its front, flipper-like limbs to pull itself along. Since its limbs had formed in water, its back legs probably weren't strong enough to support its weight on land. So this animal made its way across sand and rocks with just its front limbs.

Ichthyostega was one of the first tetrapods to make the transition from water to land. Tetrapods are animals with four limbs, including modern mammals, birds, reptiles, and amphibians. Amphibians are members of the class Amphibia, which includes extinct and modern amphibians. *Ichthyostega* is one of the earliest ancestors of modern amphibians.

Because it had the characteristics of both a fish and a tetrapod, *Ichthyostega* is known as a "fishapod." Like a fish, it had gills, small scales on its body, a dorsal fin on its tail, and ears that worked best underwater. But like a tetrapod, it had a set of lungs, a rigid skull, a strong rib cage, and large bones inside four thick limbs. Its joints—elbows, wrists, knees, and ankles—were also similar to those of tetrapods. And it had seven digits on each of its feet.

Ichthyostega lived during the Devonian period (419.2–358.9 MYA). The Devonian had a warmer climate than today. Oceans covered more than 85 percent of Earth, and landmasses were grouped into supercontinents.[2] This period is also known as the Age of Fishes because of the large variety of fish in the seas. It is when the first amphibians were born.

WHAT ARE MODERN AMPHIBIANS?

Modern amphibians are animals that can live both in water and on land. In fact, the word *amphibian* comes from the Greek *amphibious*, which means "living a double life." Most amphibians begin life in the water and move onto land at maturity.

GOLDEN POISON FROG

Many frogs produce a poison in glands of their skin to keep predators at bay. But the golden poison frog of Colombia produces one of the deadliest ones. Named for its often yellow color, it can also be orange or pale green. Measuring approximately one to two inches (2.5–5 cm) in length, it can produce enough poison to kill ten adult humans.[4]

There are more than 7,900 species of amphibians in the world, and they can be broken up into three main groups.[3] Frogs comprise the largest group, and they are of the order Anura. They have short bodies with no tails, and their hind legs are strong, longer than their front legs, and ideal for leaping. Salamanders make up the second-largest group, and they are of the order Caudata. They have tails, and their front and back limbs are about the same size. Finally, the smallest group of amphibians is called the caecilians, of the order Gymnophiona. Caecilians resemble large earthworms and have no limbs. Their bodies are ideal for burrowing.

CLASSIFICATION

Golden Poison Frog
Phyllobates terribilis

DOMAIN	**Eukaryota**. This domain includes plants, animals, and fungi. These organisms are grouped together because their cells each have a nucleus, a cell structure that contains the DNA.
KINGDOM	**Animalia**. All animals, including mammals and amphibians, are in this group.
PHYLUM	**Chordata**. Organisms in this phylum have a nerve cord down their backs supported by a rod of cartilage at some point in life. All animals with spines, including mammals and fish, are in this group.
CLASS	**Amphibia**. This class contains caecilians, frogs, and salamanders.
ORDER	**Anura**. This order contains frogs and toads.
FAMILY	**Dendrobatidae**. Frogs in this family are typically small, poisonous, and have colorful skin.
GENUS	***Phyllobates***. These small, poisonous frogs are active during the day and live in Central and South America.
SPECIES	***terribilis***. Golden poison frogs are often yellow and live in the Amazon rain forest.

Taxonomic classification is the science of identifying living things, grouping them together, and naming them. When this is done, each organism is assigned a place in eight different categories ranging from domain, the most general category, to species, the most specific category. When the scientific name of an animal is given, it includes the genus, which is capitalized, and the species, which is not. Golden poison frogs are *Phyllobates terribilis*. Scientific names are often abbreviated after first use: *P. terribilis*.

Tadpoles are the larvae of frogs.

Like birds and mammals, amphibians are vertebrates. They have a spinal column and a brain

that is part of their nervous system. Amphibians have moist skin and can breathe through the

surface of their skin. They also have glands on their skin that produce proteins. These proteins fight bacteria, move water into and out of their bodies, and help defend against predators. This defense can take the form of poison. The dart frog, for instance, produces a chemical called curare on its skin, which causes paralysis.

Most amphibians breed by laying eggs in fresh water, though some lay eggs on leaves, in damp soil, in tree holes, or in a foamy nest made from mucus. The larvae, immature versions of the adult animal, grow inside the eggs. Once the larvae hatch, they grow and develop in the water away from the adults of their species. They must find their own food and evade predators on their own. Larvae mainly eat plants, and the adults eat other animals.

As the larvae mature, they go through a metamorphosis, or change, from aquatic animals to terrestrial, or land based, animals. Most grow limbs and develop lungs. Once this is complete, most amphibians leave the water to live on the land.

Amphibians cannot regulate their own body temperature internally, so this means they are always the same temperature as their environment. If the environment is cold, they are cold. If it's hot, they're hot. In addition, too much sun can damage their cells, and too much wind can dehydrate them. For this reason, amphibians are more sensitive to changes in the environment than many other animals.

EVOLUTION

How did an animal like *Ichthyostega* become a modern amphibian? The answer lies in evolution. Evolution is the scientific theory that all life on Earth changes over time. All life on Earth evolved from microorganisms that lived billions of years ago. Across countless generations and hundreds of millions of years, these life-forms evolved into the species we see today. Throughout Earth's history, these changes have taken place across countless generations and hundreds of millions of years. All modern plants, animals, insects, and other organisms evolved from common ancestors that lived billions of years ago.

EVOLUTION OF DIGITS

Approximately 340 MYA, tetrapods started walking rather than swimming. Walking required feet that could balance and push off varying surfaces. Ankles and wrists needed to move in new ways as well. As these joints changed, so did the number of digits on hands and feet. Today, most animals have just five digits, though some have fewer.[6] Why five? Scientists aren't sure, but they do know that species tend to lose digits over time and almost never gain new ones.

Charles Darwin was an influential scientist in studying evolution. From 1831 to 1836, he sailed around the world on the HMS *Beagle*. As a naturalist, he became fascinated with fossil bones in Argentina and animals he observed on the Galapagos Islands in Ecuador. He took more than 1,700 pages of notes and kept a 770-page diary.[5] When he came home to the United Kingdom, he studied his notes and performed

People around the
world are familiar
with Charles
Darwin's research
on evolution.

Scientists are using many tools and methods to learn about amphibian evolution.

experiments for many years. He also read a book about human populations. This book said that when a population of humans increased, people struggled over a limited number of resources. The ones that were the most fit survived the competition for resources. Darwin applied this to the natural world and called it natural selection. He said that plants and animals struggled and endured through harsh environments and predators. Those who survived passed their traits on to the next generation. He published a book about this in 1859 called *On the Origin of the Species*. It was a breakthrough in the scientific community.

Today, scientists study evolution in many ways. They examine the fossil record to understand extinct organisms or observe how a species changed over time. They compare the skeletons of different animals to find similarities and differences. They look at how organisms develop before the organisms hatch or are born, because some features in embryos can give clues as to the evolution of a species. Scientists also study how and why plants and animals have moved across the Earth in the past. This science is called biogeography. It aims to explain these movements during the evolution of organisms by studying Earth's history, including the movement of continents, rise of mountains, and appearance of new rivers. Finally, scientists look at the molecular biology of organisms. DNA, genes, and other microscopic clues tell about the ancestors of a species.

BIOGEOGRAPHY

In biogeography, scientists study why certain animals live in particular places. For instance, Hawaii has approximately one-third of all the species of vinegar flies in the world. Why so many in such a small place? It isn't the environment. Other tropical islands are just as suitable for vinegar flies, yet they don't have the same number, if they have any at all. The same applies to other animals, such as zebras in Africa or kangaroos in Australia.

Evolution provides an explanation. If all species of flies evolved from one ancestor, then the only way vinegar flies appeared on Hawaii was if they evolved from an ancestor that had arrived from the nearby continent once these volcanic islands emerged from the ocean. The same holds true with kangaroos in Australia. Kangaroos are related to other marsupial mammals that arrived millions of years ago in what is now Australia. While they have existed for millions of years, they have not had the opportunity to spread to other continents due to deepwater ocean barriers that they cannot cross. However, they have managed to colonize nearby New Guinea, probably at times when these two large islands were connected by land.

CHAPTER TWO

Becoming Tetrapods

The South American lungfish is one of the only species of lobe-finned fish alive today.

The ancestors of tetrapods once lived in the sea. Approximately 400 MYA, in the Devonian, the earliest tetrapod ancestors were fish. Specifically, they were a type of fish called a lobe-finned fish. A lobe is a curved or rounded projection of a body part, such as the lobe of an ear. In lobe-finned fish, the fins were the lobes. The fins were different from those of the most common type of fish today, the ray-finned fish. Ray-finned fish make up about 96 percent of all fish species. Their fins connect to their bodies with several small bones.[1] From these bones, a row of long, thin bones fan out and are covered in a webbing. Lobe-finned fish fins are connected to the body with a single bone.

Muscles and skin cover the fin bones. These fins with skin and muscle had the potential to support the animal on land. Eventually, these lobe fins evolved into arms and legs.

LOBE-FINNED FISH

The sarcopterygian fish were the lobe-finned ancestors of tetrapods. Most scientists believe one sarcopterygian, the extinct Panderichthyidae, may be an ancestor of the tetrapods. Sarcopterygians probably developed their limbs in the water because the water supported their weight. This allowed flexible elbow, wrist, knee, and ankle joints to grow more easily. When the animal crawled onto land, these joints helped it wade in shallow water or push through dense vegetation. Gravity then forced it to grow a sturdier skeleton with a rigid spinal column and flexible vertebrae. It also developed a hip girdle to connect the legs to the backbone, and a shoulder girdle to attach the arms to the neck. On land, muscles grew and strengthened.

In addition to limbs, the sarcopterygians had to develop their lungs. In order to breathe while in the water, they would rise to the surface and gulp in some air. As they dove back down, water pressure forced the air back into their lungs, which exchanged oxygen for carbon dioxide. Then, as sarcopterygians rose again, the reduced water pressure pushed the carbon dioxide out of their lungs and into their mouths. They would release it when they reached the surface and

Coelacanths used to be widespread, but today scientists know of only two living species of these lobe-finned fish.

gulped in more air. Eventually, their muscles developed, and they didn't need water pressure to breathe. They could control their breathing with muscles, allowing them to spend time on land.

Sarcopterygians developed in other ways. Their necks became flexible so they could reach down and pick up food from the ground rather than scoop it out of the water. Their skin grew tough to protect them from friction as they moved over sharp rocks and through rough vegetation. Their skin also changed to prevent them from drying out in the hot sun. Sarcopterygians developed sensory organs of sight, hearing, and smell. In the water, they could use vibrations around them to sense food or predators, but on land, they had to rely on other senses.

Experts disagree on why the lobe-finned fish made the change from water to land. Perhaps they started looking for food in shallow water and used their limbs to move around. Or perhaps,

ROMER'S GAP

In the 1950s, Harvard professor Alfred Sherwood Romer discovered a 15-million-year gap in the fossil record. This period was a mystery for scientists. Some scientists believed that oxygen levels in the atmosphere were too low for tetrapods to move to land. Others believed there was a mass extinction event. Still others, including evolution scientist Jennifer Clack, believed people just weren't looking in the right places.

Willie's Hole in Scotland yielded a big find. In 2015, scientists from the National Museum of Scotland found fossils at Willie's Hole from the Romer's Gap time period. In a riverbed, they dug up diverse tetrapods with a wide range of body types. One large fossil, dubbed Ribbo because of its prominent ribs, showed that tetrapods were able to thrive during the gap. This indicates that oxygen levels weren't too low for tetrapods to move out of the water as previously thought. Other fossils showed well-developed lungs but limbs that were still too weak to support the animal's weight on land. They probably walked by dragging their bodies along the ground. These fossils suggest that the gap may not exist at all and that more fossils are still to be found.

as the climate grew drier, they had to crawl from one pool of water to the next as each one evaporated in the sun. Or perhaps larger predators chased them out of the water to an area dense with vegetation.

The changes happened very slowly. In fact, it took approximately 80 million years for lobe-finned fish to adapt from water to land. With current evidence, it is hard for scientists to get a good picture of how this transition occurred. This is because of a large gap in the fossil record between 360 and 345 MYA called Romer's Gap. Before the gap, scientists have found many fossils of transition animals. Fossils before the gap have a mixture of fish and tetrapod features. After the gap, they found fossils of tetrapods that lived on land. These fossils show tetrapod features only. Some fossils from the gap have been found, but more need to be uncovered before a clear picture can be formed.

TRANSITION ANIMALS

As animals changed, or transitioned, from fish to tetrapods, they had features of both. Two of the earliest of these transition animals are *Eusthenopteron* and *Panderichthys*. These lobe-finned fish lived from approximately 385 to 380 MYA and were three feet (1 m) long.[2] They had large mouths, pointed heads, and bodies that were wide in the middle and narrow at the ends. Their short fins had bones that spread outward and showed the potential to develop into limbs.

Another possible transition animal is *Tiktaalik*. Partial and complete skeletons were discovered in northern Canada in 2004, and some scientists believe it is a missing link between fish and amphibians. But most believe that, although it may be an example of an animal that evolved from living in the water to living on land for at least some of the time, it is not a direct link to modern amphibians. It might be a distant cousin to amphibians instead.

Tiktaalik lived 375 MYA and grew to approximately ten feet (3 m) in length with a body like a crocodile.[3] It lived in shallow fresh water, such as streams or swamps. Similar to a fish, it had scales and fins, but its front fins had primitive shoulder, elbow, and wrist joints, which helped it walk on land. It had a distinct neck that allowed it to move its head separately from its body as a modern tetrapod does. Its upper jaw connected to its skull in a way that suggested it could sometimes breathe without using its gills.

EARLIEST TETRAPODS

The primitive tetrapods *Ichthyostega* and *Acanthostega* lived later in the Devonian, approximately 370–360 MYA. Fossils of both animals were found in Greenland. Gunnar Säve-Söderbergh, a geologist from Denmark, discovered *Ichthyostega* in 1931. And Dr. Jennifer Clack, a British expert on tetrapod evolution, discovered more-complete *Acanthostega* fossils in 1987.

When Säve-Söderbergh discovered *Ichthyostega*, he didn't find a complete skeleton. He found a flat skull that looked like it belonged on a lobe-finned fish. Yet it had a snout like an early tetrapod. At the time, no tetrapod fossils had ever been found that dated to before 300 MYA. But as Säve-Söderbergh examined the skull, he realized he'd found a fossil from 60 million years before that. It was the earliest fossil of a tetrapod in existence. Later, other scientists went back to Greenland over the course of many years. They discovered a tail, legs, and shoulders of *Ichthyostega* and were able to form a more complete model.

The picture that emerged was of a squat animal approximately three feet long (1 m) with a short snout, small scales, and a dorsal fin on its upper back, like that of a fish.[4] It also had lungs, limbs, strong ribs, and ankle, knee, wrist, and elbow joints. There were seven digits on its hind feet. Its tail was a mixture of that of a fish and a tetrapod.[5]

In 1987, Clack set out to find fossils in Greenland. For six weeks, she camped out in bitterly cold weather and hiked four hours each day to a fossil bed. She was looking for *Acanthostega* specimens. Before then, only two pieces of skull had been found, and Clack wanted to see how transitional tetrapods, such as *Acanthostega*, had moved from water to land. The scientific consensus at that time was that lobe-finned fish had left the water and then developed limbs. But Clack wasn't sure that was right.

"As the sun glanced across the specimen in Greenland," she said, "we could see the bones and we thought, 'Aha! There's something in there,' but we had no idea how good it

FINDING A SKULL

In 1931, Gunnar Säve-Söderbergh explored Greenland as part of a Danish expedition. Mostly, he found familiar lobe-finned fish fossils, but he also found pieces of a skull he couldn't identify. He thought it probably belonged to a type of amphibian. But back home in Sweden, he dug the pieces out of the sandstone and put them together like a puzzle. What he saw was not an amphibian or a lobe-finned fish, but something else—the earliest tetrapod. He named it *Ichthyostega*, which means "fish plate," because of the shape of its skull. The public loved this discovery, and one newspaper even created a cartoon about it.

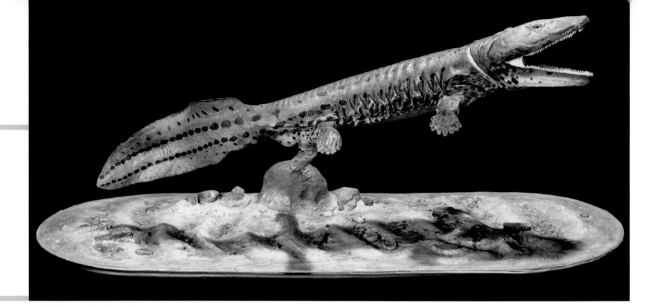

Models show people what ancient tetrapods, including *Acanthostega*, may have looked like.

was going to be."[6] She took the fossil back to the United Kingdom. After the nearly complete skeleton was carefully chipped away from the surrounding rock, she was able to get the first real picture of *Acanthostega*. Its arms had eight digits, not five as she'd expected. It had a fishlike tail and gills. And its wrist joints were too weak to have supported its body weight on land. Neither *Ichthyostega* nor *Acanthostega* could have walked on land with its weak hind legs. So it must have been developing legs while still in the water. Clack's discovery overturned scientific thinking about how tetrapods left the water. Scientists now believe lobe-finned fish developed limbs before, not after, they left the water. This animal probably spent most of its time in water. *Acanthostega* had both fish and tetrapod features, with gills and backward-pointing legs. More than three feet (1 m) long, it had eight fingers on its front feet, and its teeth showed that it obtained some of its food from the land.[7]

Another primitive tetrapod, *Pederpes*, existed approximately 350 MYA. Norwegian paleontologist Peder Aspen discovered it in 1971. Aspen found the almost-complete skeleton in limestone rocks in Dumbarton, Scotland. Three feet (1 m) long, *Pederpes* had a head shaped like a triangle.[8] Its sense organs were along the side of its body, and its middle ear indicated that it spent a lot of time in the water. However, its hind feet and wrist and ankle joints indicated that it was fully adapted to life on land.

At first, Aspen thought *Pederpes* was a lobe-finned fish. But later, Clack examined it and realized *Pederpes* was actually a primitive tetrapod. In fact, most scientists believe that *Pederpes* is the first terrestrial tetrapod in the

FOSSILS

Scientists study fossils such as *Ichthyostega*, *Tiktaalik*, and *Pederpes* using many methods. One way is mechanically. Scientists carefully chip away at rocks with needles, drills, compressed air, or other tools to expose the fossil buried within. And they clean the surface with chemicals. But scientists also use computed tomography (CT) scanning. From the scan, scientists can create digital images and print out three-dimensional (3-D) models. One fossil called Tiny was never removed from its rock. Yet scientists were able to use 3-D scanning and printing to create a replica of the animal (pictured). What they found was an important fossil from the Romer's Gap time period, a small female with teeth. Because it is still encased within the rock, this fossil has yet to be seen directly by human eyes.

fossil record. And because it existed during Romer's Gap, it provides information on tetrapod development during that time period.

DEVONIAN ENVIRONMENT

During the Devonian, the planet underwent significant changes. Major landmasses moved in a process called plate tectonics. The supercontinent Gondwana headed north and away from the South Pole. The landmasses that today form North America, Russia, Greenland, and northern Europe moved toward each other to form the supercontinent Laurasia.

The Devonian is called the Age of Fishes because of the rich diversity of fish that appeared in the fossil record at that time. For instance, the placoderms appeared during the Devonian. These fish had armor, had jaws with plates instead of teeth, and grew up to 33 feet (10 m) in length.[9] Other types of fish had

PLATE TECTONICS

Plate tectonics is a theory that describes the movement of plates on Earth. Plates are landmasses both above and below water, and they make up the outer layer of Earth. This outer layer is called the lithosphere, and it floats atop a molten layer of rock. The molten layer has currents that force the plates above it to move around. At boundaries where the plates meet, they interact in three different ways. They can move toward each other, they can move away from each other, and they can slide past each other. Volcanoes, earthquakes, and mountains result from these movements.

Shark ancestors lived during the Devonian.

heads in the shape of horseshoes or bodies like round shields. Ancestors of today's fish included cartilaginous fish and bony fish. Cartilaginous fish had cartilage instead of bones. Eventually, they became the sharks and rays of today. Bony fish had bones. They included lobe-finned fish and species similar to modern fish.

On land, plants evolved and spread from wetlands to drier regions as they adapted to new environments. Trees grew strong trunks that could support branches and leaves, and some grew to more than 100 feet (30 m) tall.[10] Forests expanded across the land and included horsetails, ferns, and seed plants.

CHAPTER THREE

Ancient Amphibians

Some tetrapods began displaying traits similar to modern amphibians approximately 310 to 300 MYA in the late part of the Carboniferous period (358.9–298.9 MYA). They were a diverse group of animals that did not resemble modern frogs, salamanders, or caecilians. Some grew to be more than 20 feet (6 m) in length.[1] Others never reached six inches (15 cm).[2] Some lived mostly in the water, while others stayed mostly on land. This Age of Amphibians, as it is called, lasted until 260 MYA at the end of the Permian period (298.9–251.9 MYA). At that time, oxygen levels rose close to today's level, and the Earth became more arid, causing many ancient amphibians to die out. At this time, many of the major groups

Fossils of ancient amphibians have helped scientists learn about these creatures.

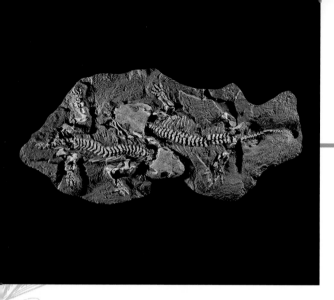

SEYMOURIA

In 1906, a short, compact fossil was found in the town of Seymour, Texas. Named after the town, *Seymouria* was first thought to be a reptile because it had dry skin and an ability to conserve water in an arid climate. It could also live out of the water for long periods of time and excrete salt through a gland in its nose. As other fossils of *Seymouria* were found in New Mexico, Oklahoma, Utah, and Germany, scientists determined that *Seymouria* wasn't a reptile. It was an amphibian with reptilelike traits.

of amniotes appeared, including reptiles and mammals.

CHARACTERISTICS

Like their modern counterparts, females of these amphibian-like tetrapods laid eggs in water. When the eggs hatched, larvae emerged. These were immature versions of the adult animal, similar to tadpoles in modern frogs. The larvae stayed in the water and breathed through gills. As they matured, they went through metamorphosis, where they lost their gills and developed lungs and limbs. Adults often looked quite different from their larvae.

After metamorphosis, the adults moved onto land and used their lungs to breathe. Most of them had slimy skin that could absorb

TETRAPODS DIVERSIFY

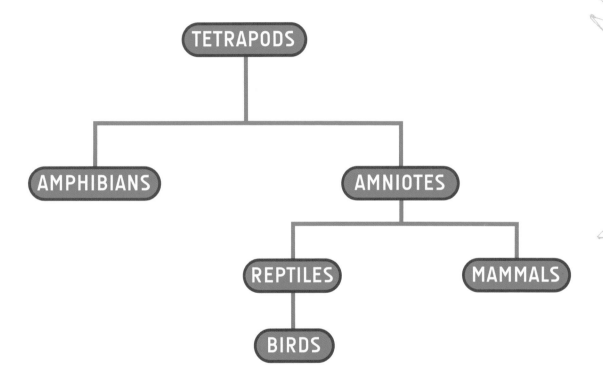

Millions of years ago, the ancestor to all modern amphibians diverged from tetrapods. Other creatures, called amniotes, also diverged from tetrapods. Amniotes became the ancestors to modern mammals, reptiles, and eventually, birds.

additional oxygen into their bloodstream. Large ancient amphibians ate smaller amphibians and reptiles. Smaller amphibians ate fish and insects such as flies and beetles.

The diversity of ancient amphibians included many different species. Colosteids were small animals that lived in the water and had long bodies and well-developed limbs. Microsaurs resembled small salamanders. They had well-developed arms and legs that were small compared to the rest of their bodies. They grew to less than six inches (15 cm) in length. The aistopods had bodies with no limbs, like modern caecilians. They grew to be 39 inches (99 cm) long.[3] They may have lived in the water or on land, but they probably were not burrowing animals as modern caecilians are. Their skulls were too fragile. Scientists disagree, however, on whether aistopods were ancient amphibians. Some believe aistopods may be descended from an unrelated animal.

AMPHIBIAN GROUPS

Most ancient amphibians can be separated into two groups: temnospondyls and lepospondyls. Experts disagree on which group was the ancestor of modern amphibians, but most believe it was the temnospondyls. In general, the temnospondyls were larger and more aggressive than the lepospondyls. They had divided vertebrae, big heads with flat skulls, and large jaws full of teeth. Their bodies were long and muscular, and their limbs short and stocky. Their dry, scaly skin was probably a reaction to the dry climate of the Permian and a way to prevent dehydration. They lived in freshwater lakes and rivers and usually resembled crocodiles.

Eogyrinus and *Eryops*, both examples of temnospondyls, lived approximately 300 MYA. *Eogyrinus* grew up to 15 feet (4.5 m) in length and lived in swamps.[4] *Eryops* grew to approximately 6.5 feet (2 m) and had a strong spine and limbs. *Mastodonsaurus* was a giant temnospondyl with a head 6.5 feet (2 m) long and a body about double that size.[5] *Fedexia* was a two-foot (60 cm) carnivorous temnospondyl that had adapted fully to land.[6] It lived 300 MYA and was one of the first amphibians to move onto land. It probably resembled a salamander. Its sharp teeth indicate that it was a carnivore.

The lepospondyls were smaller than the temnospondyls, and most had skulls less than two inches (5 cm) in length.[7] They had fragile

TEETH

Temnospondyls had fang-like teeth around the edges of their mouths. But they also had thousands of small barb-like teeth all over the roofs of their mouths, or palates. Called denticles, these tiny barbs were common in tetrapods. However, they were usually just on the hard part of the palate. Temnospondyls had them on both the hard and soft parts of the palates. They were probably used to grab prey, such as smaller amphibians and other animals, and hold on to them as they ate.

FEDEXIA

In 2004, college junior Adam Striegel went on a geology class field trip near the Pittsburgh, Pennsylvania, airport. He picked up a softball-sized rock that looked like the fossil of a fern. The rock was cumbersome, though, so Striegel tossed it aside. He later changed his mind and showed it to his professor.

What Striegel had found wasn't a rock. It was a skull. And the shapes he thought were fern fronds were teeth. With this exciting find, Striegel and his professor went to the Carnegie Museum of Natural History. They showed the skull to David Berman, curator of paleontology. Berman recognized the skull as a trematopid, a type of temnospondyl. But it wasn't like any trematopid ever seen before. It was a brand-new species. "I have had five to 10 great discoveries in my 40-year career, and you live for those moments," Berman said. "The only thing that could be better is if I had made the discovery myself."[9]

The fossil was named *Fedexia striegeli*— "Fedexia" after the company that owned the land where it was found and "striegeli" for the student who found it.

skeletons, spool-shaped vertebrae, and lived both in water and on land. Like modern frogs, they had moist, slimy skin. They were probably the most common land vertebrates during the Age of Amphibians.

Microbrachis, a lepospondyl that lived on the European landmass approximately 300 MYA, had small, well-developed limbs. It grew to less than six inches (15 cm) in length and looked like a modern salamander.[8] Snakelike *Ophiderpeton* was similar to a modern caecilian.

Lepospondyls were known for their odd appearance, and one of the oddest was *Diplocaulus*. It lived 270 MYA and was one of the larger amphibians in the Permian. It grew to approximately three feet (1 m) in length. *Diplocaulus* had short limbs and a flat body, and

Diplocaulus swam in lakes and other bodies of water.

it spent most of its time in the water. The most remarkable feature of *Diplocaulus* was its large, triangular head, about one foot (30 cm) across.[10] It was shaped like a boomerang. Scientists speculate that the head protected the animal from predators because it was too big to eat. Or perhaps the boomerang shape reduced resistance underwater, similar to how the wings of an airplane reduce drag in the air. *Diplocaulus* also had eyes on the top of its head, indicating that it spent a lot of time on the bottoms of rivers and swamps. As food swam nearby, it probably leaped up and caught prey in its strong jaws.

CARBONIFEROUS AND PERMIAN ENVIRONMENT

When ancient amphibians appeared approximately 310 MYA, in the late part of the Carboniferous, the land was covered with swampy forests. These forests were the first to exist on Earth. Large trees grew there, along with club mosses, tree ferns, and seedless trees called calamites.

Giant cockroaches, similar to the ones living today but up to three feet (1 m) long, roamed the forests. Centipedes grew up to six feet (2 m), and dragonflies had wingspans up to 2.5 feet (0.75 m).[11] This time period is called the Golden Age of Sharks because there were so many sharks in the ocean. In addition, a jawless fish called the lamprey lived in the ocean, along with an invertebrate called a crinoid.

The level of oxygen in the atmosphere during the Carboniferous was much higher than it is today. It made up 35 percent of the air as compared to today's 21 percent.[12] The massive forests pulled carbon dioxide from the atmosphere and used photosynthesis to release oxygen back into the air. As trees with bark died, they became peat, a type of decomposed soil that can be used for fuel. Eventually, the peat deposits turned into coal, which is made of carbon. The name *Carboniferous* comes from this process.

As they had during the Devonian, continents continued to move during the

PERMIAN EXTINCTION

Approximately 250 MYA, the worst extinction event in Earth's history occurred at the end of the Permian period. More than 70 percent of land animals and more than 90 percent of sea creatures died out.[13] Why did this happen? No one is sure. Perhaps a series of volcanic eruptions threw massive amounts of ash and debris into the air. This blocked the sun so plants couldn't make oxygen from photosynthesis. As the plants died out, so did the animals that ate them. Or perhaps an earthquake released methane gas from the seafloor. Toxic levels of carbon dioxide in the oceans could also have been involved. Or maybe the climate experienced a sudden warming and cooling. No matter the cause, it created a major change to life on the planet.

Carboniferous and Permian. The supercontinent of Laurasia in the north drifted toward Gondwana in the south, and by the end of the Permian, they had combined to form one gigantic supercontinent called Pangaea. Because this continent was so large, it featured diverse climates. In the south, it was cold and dry, with much of the land frozen. In the north, it could be extremely hot, with both wet and dry seasons.

During the Permian, the forests became drier. Conifers, ferns, seed plants, and other life adapted to the more arid conditions. The dominant animal was no longer the amphibian. It was the reptile. One group of reptiles, the therapsids, were the most common. They had characteristics of both mammals and reptiles and could be either carnivores or herbivores. In the oceans lived bony fish that had thick scales and fan-shaped fins. Nautiloids, animals that looked like squids, lived in reefs. Ammonoids, with their spiral shells, also thrived. By the end of the Permian, the climate had changed so much that most life on the planet died out. The Permian extinction was the most severe extinction event in Earth's history.

Ammonoid fossils
are commonly found
in rock.

How Metamorphosis Evolved

Modern frogs, salamanders, and caecilians all have species that undergo metamorphosis. In most species, the female lays eggs that hatch into larvae. The larvae live in water and change into adults. Then the young adults leave the water to live on land. But why would any animal develop such a complicated way of growing up?

The answer lies in their diet—specifically, in the change from a fish-based diet to an insect-based diet. From the fossil record, scientists know that most temnospondyls that lived in the water ate fish. However, two types of temnospondyls, the amphibamid and zatracheid, had small teeth, and their tongue structures were different from those of other amphibians of the time period. This suggested that they ate prey on land and used their tongues to do so. Some amphibamids also had teeth that looked like those in modern amphibians. Scientists believe that for these ancient amphibians to change from a water-based diet to a land-based diet, they needed to evolve quickly. Those who did so were more likely to survive. This rapid change became metamorphosis.

In addition, having a smaller body size would make the transition faster. This could explain why today's amphibians are much smaller than the ancient temnospondyls. And it could also explain why the salamanders of today that do not undergo or fully complete metamorphosis, such as sirens and giant salamanders, are also large.

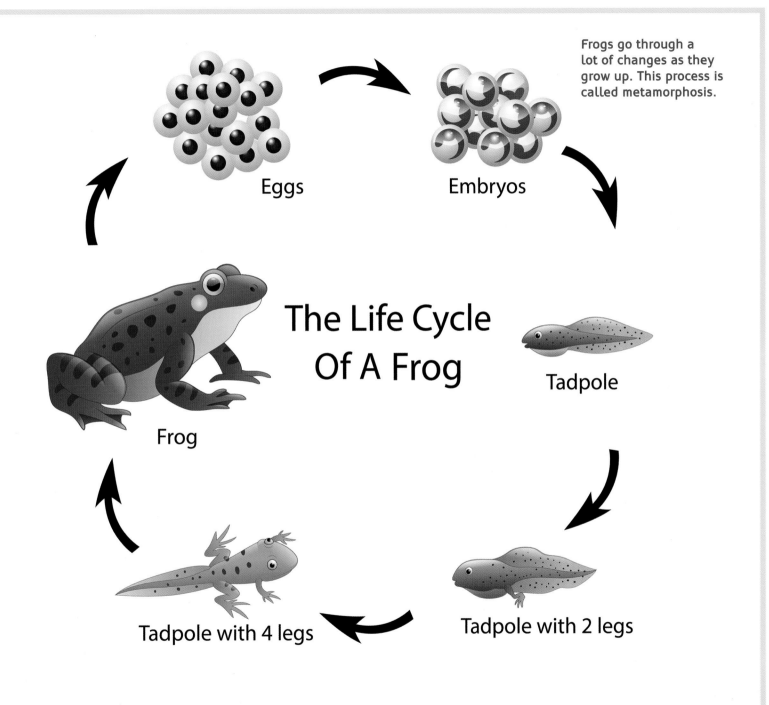

The Life Cycle Of A Frog

Eggs

Embryos

Frogs go through a lot of changes as they grow up. This process is called metamorphosis.

Tadpole

Tadpole with 2 legs

Tadpole with 4 legs

Frog

CHAPTER FOUR

Early Frogs

When the Permian period ended, the earliest chapter of life on Earth came to a close. This had been the time of primitive life on Earth, the time when all life began. Now the next phase was beginning: the time of middle life, which included the Triassic period (251.9–201.3 MYA), Jurassic period (201.3–145 MYA), and Cretaceous period (145–66 MYA). This is called the Mesozoic era. It is famous for dinosaurs roaming the land. It is also when the first modern amphibians were born.

POSSIBLE RELATIVES

Modern amphibians belong to a class called lissamphibians. *Liss* means "smooth" in Latin, a reference to lissamphibians' smooth skin. Lissamphibians began appearing in the middle part of the

Amphibamus is one of several ancient relatives to modern amphibians.

Triassic, between 252 and 201 MYA. Many scientists believe they had one common ancestor, though experts do not all agree on this ancestor's identity. One possible ancient ancestor is *Amphibamus*, a temnospondyl that lived 300 MYA. It had a wide skull and grew to eight inches (20 cm) in length.[1] It lived in the swamps of North America and Europe.

LISSAMPHIBIAN CHARACTERISTICS

Lissamphibians share several characteristics unique to them. For instance, they have moist skin used for absorbing water and for breathing along with their lungs. They have two sense receptors in their inner ear. Their eyes contain green rods to let them tell different hues apart. They have small two-part teeth attached to the inner side of their jaw. They also have short ribs and unique elbow joints. Glands in their mouths create a sticky substance that drops onto their tongues and allows them to capture and hang on to prey. Because so many of these features relate to the soft tissues of the body instead of the skeleton, it has been difficult to identify the ancient relatives of lissamphibians in the fossil record.

A possible relative is *Gerobatrachus*. Scientists believe it is most closely related to frogs and salamanders. When it was discovered in Texas in 2008, the press called it a "frogamander" because it had a head like a frog and a tail like a salamander. *Gerobatrachus* lived 290 MYA and grew to be 4.5 inches (11 cm) long.[2] Because it shared characteristics of both frogs and salamanders, scientists speculated that frogs and salamanders both evolved from temnospondyls. The odd-looking caecilians, with no limbs, might have evolved from lepospondyls.

A third relative for lissamphibians was *Triadobatrachus massinoti*. It is most closely related to frogs. In 1930, Adrien Massinot discovered the fossil on Madagascar, an island off the southeastern coast of Africa. Then in 1936, French paleontologist Jean Piveteau studied it. He determined that *T. massinoti* had lived 250 MYA and was an early ancestor of the modern frog. It was a transitional animal with both ancient and modern frog traits. He named the animal, in part, after Massinot.

Piveteau was able to study *T. massinoti* so thoroughly because he had the majority of the bones of the four-inch- (10 cm) long animal.[3] Not only that but the limbs were also in the correct anatomical positions. This means that

MADAGASCAR

Madagascar is a hotbed of fossils (pictured). Stony Brook University's Department of Anatomical Sciences has conducted ten years of research on the island. Scientists found more than 550 specimens in one year alone.[4] They include everything from frogs, snakes, and turtles to birds, mammals, and dinosaurs. The fossil-rich nature of the island is due in part to the weather. During the Cretaceous, the climate had rainy seasons that lasted weeks or months. The massive amounts of rain caused debris to flow down from the highlands to the region that eventually became Madagascar. The moving debris picked up skeletons and dead animals, entombing them quickly and depositing them in fields. This rapid burial preserved them for millions of years.

Triadobatrachus massinoti, bottom, resembled a modern frog in several ways.

the animal had been preserved quickly before it could be eaten by prey or washed away by the environment. Piveteau could study it in its original form.

From his examination, Piveteau found that the animal had a short body and broad head like a modern frog. But unlike modern frogs, the radius and ulna, the long bones of the forearm, were not fused. Nor were the tibia and fibula, the bones of the lower leg. Plus, *T. massinoti* still had its tail, which modern frogs absorb during metamorphosis.

In addition, *T. massinoti* had long hind legs and anklebones. This suggested that it might have been able to jump on land like modern frogs, but further evidence indicated that it could not do so. The rocks in which *T. massinoti* had been found came from the sea, not the land. This indicates that *T. massinoti* probably spent most of its life in water and used its powerful hind legs for swimming rather than jumping.

FIRST ANCESTRAL FROGS

Vieraella lived approximately 200 MYA. Many experts believe it was the first amphibian with the characteristics of a modern frog. It was a tiny animal, measuring just one inch (2.5 cm) long and weighing less than one ounce (28 g).[5] Like modern frogs, it had large eyes and muscular legs, and it resembled modern frogs.

Another ancestral frog was *Prosalirus bitis*. Like *Vieraella*, it lived about 200 MYA. Its fossil was discovered in 1981 in Arizona by Harvard professor Farish Jenkins. What was remarkable about *P. bitis* was that it was the first ancestral frog in the fossil record believed to be able to jump.

It had several features that made jumping possible. The largest bone in its pelvis, the ilium, was longer than the same bone in its ancestor, *T. massinoti*. Plus, the vertebrae in the tail region of *P. bitis* were fused together into what is called a urostyle. This is similar to modern frogs. Together, the ilium and urostyle formed a structure in the pelvis that is common in modern frogs. This structure is strong and inflexible. Combining this with long legs and anklebones, *P. bitis* probably could jump just as well as modern frogs, using its strong legs not just in the water but also on land. In fact, the name *Prosalirus* means "jump forward."

As the Jurassic progressed into the Cretaceous, ancestral frogs evolved, becoming similar to modern frogs. An example of this evolution is *Enneabatrachus*. It lived approximately 150 MYA and was the ancestor of modern midwife toads and painted frogs. Another example is a giant frog, *Beelzebufo ampinga*, found on Madagascar that dates to 70 MYA. This frog may be closely related to a frog that lives in South America today.

While modern frogs are well known for their jumping abilities, early frogs did not all have this ability.

GIANT FROG

Beelzebufo ampinga was a giant frog that lived about 70 MYA. Scientists first discovered evidence of it in 1998 when they found a small piece of bone. Several years and many more pieces later, Susan Evans from University College London puzzled it together.

B. ampinga, which means "devil frog," was the size of a beach ball. It measured 16 inches (41 cm) tall and weighed ten pounds (4.5 kg).[6] It is believed to be a close relative of the modern-day members of the *Ceratophrys* genus that live in South America. Because of the two creatures' similarities, scientists believe that *B. ampinga* was probably just as aggressive as *Ceratophrys* frogs. To eat, it probably just sat around and snatched with its powerful jaws any food that wandered by, perhaps including baby dinosaurs.

ANCIENT ENVIRONMENT

What was the world like for the ancestors of the modern frog? When the Triassic began, Earth was still recovering from the Permian extinction event. With most species gone, there were opportunities for the remaining life to evolve into new forms to replace those that had gone extinct. At this time, other groups of vertebrates evolved, most notably dinosaurs and mammals about 230 MYA.

The supercontinent Pangaea was starting to break apart during the Triassic. Coastal areas experienced monsoons while the interior stayed warm and dry. During the Jurassic, North America and Eurasia split apart from Laurasia. The eastern half of Gondwana split from Africa and South America. Oceans expanded to fill the

CONTINENTAL DRIFT

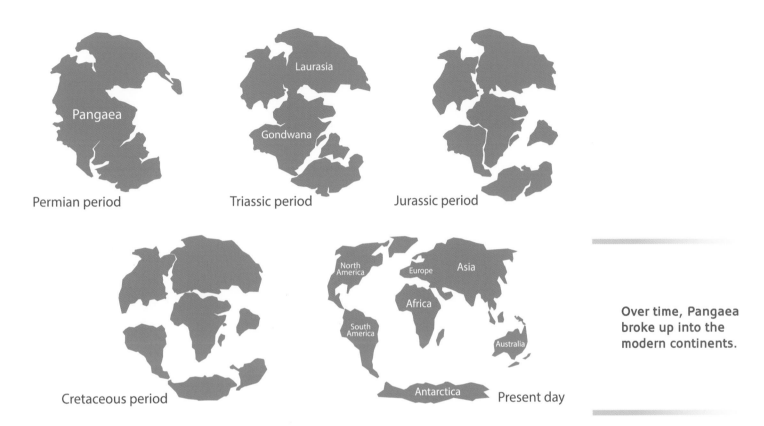

Permian period

Triassic period

Jurassic period

Cretaceous period

Present day

Over time, Pangaea broke up into the modern continents.

gaps between landmasses as new coastlines formed. This water cooled the climate across all landmasses. By the end of the Mesozoic era, the continents looked much like they do today.

Forests thrived throughout the Mesozoic. Plants including conifers, ginkgoes, and cycads filled these forests, along with mosses, liverworts, and ferns. By the end of the era, flowering plants had spread everywhere, aided by insects such as bees, wasps, ants, and beetles. Sea life

Ferns thrived during
the Cretaceous.

continued to diversify. Ammonites, mollusks, and sea urchins existed. The first coral reefs appeared, and so did sponges and snails. Giant crocodiles, sharks, and rays lived in the water.

In the skies, the first birds appeared between 201 and 145 MYA. By the end of the Cretaceous, the ancestors to cormorants, pelicans, and sandpipers existed. On the ground lived early mammals, snakes, frogs, and salamanders. At the end of this period, another extinction event occurred. Many species died out, perhaps from a large meteor striking Earth and causing worldwide harm.

METEORITE EVIDENCE

For many years, scientists wondered how the extinction event at the end of the Cretaceous occurred. In 1980, they discovered a layer of iridium, a rare element, in sedimentary clay. The clay had formed 65 MYA, the same time as the Cretaceous extinction event. But how did the iridium get there? It is common in space. Perhaps a meteorite had crashed into Earth and deposited the iridium. But skeptics wondered, if a meteorite had caused the extinction event, where was the crater?

In 1991, as researchers studied a massive crater on Yucatán Peninsula in Mexico, they thought they found the answer. Located near the town of Chicxulub, the crater was 110 miles (180 km) in diameter.[7] After much work, researchers were able to calculate the age of the crater at 65 million years old. It was such a large crater that the impact of a meteorite would've released the energy of 100 trillion short tons (90 trillion metric tons) of TNT, strong enough to cause a cataclysmic event.[8] Today, most scientists believe the Chicxulub crater is ground zero for the extinction event at the end of the Cretaceous.

Frogs have become
a diverse group
of amphibians.

CHAPTER FIVE

Modern Frogs

When the Cretaceous ended, 70 percent of all species on Earth died out.[1] Into this void surged other species. They evolved and grew at a rapid rate to repopulate the planet. This is called filling an ecological niche. An ecological niche is the slot or function that a species fills in the environment. For instance, a niche includes what a species feeds on, what feeds on it, and the role it plays in its ecological community. It includes the tools a species uses to gather food in a particular environment, such as a pointy beak or a sticky tongue. It also describes how a species interacts with the temperature, terrain, and predators, as well as how it adapts to competition or lack of resources. No two species have the exact same niche. And natural selection encourages them to be more specialized rather than less. This is because the more specialized the species, the less competition

Frogs use their sticky tongues to help catch prey.

there is for survival. And after the Cretaceous, with few dinosaurs to compete with frogs, frogs diversified and spread throughout the world.

AN EXPLOSION OF FROGS

Scientists used to think modern frogs evolved slowly, much like their ancient relatives had. They believed modern frogs appeared 150 MYA and continued evolving until 66 MYA. And they believed modern frogs all came from ancient relatives. However, new data suggests otherwise.

In 2017, scientists from four universities in the United States and China created a new large collection of genetic information for frogs. Together, they gathered new gene data from 145 frog species on hand, and they sampled genes from an additional 156 frog species.[2]

With this information, they put together a family tree called a phylogeny. A phylogeny is the history of an animal's evolution, including its ancestors. Scientists put together a family tree by looking at the fossil record and studying the genes and DNA. Scientists also look for both similarities and differences in species in how they react to their environments.

The frog family tree showed how the 55 families of living frogs are related to one another. Scientists then looked at the fossil records.[3] They wanted to know exactly when frog ancestors split from one another so they could add those dates to the tree. Had the ancestors split gradually, as always thought? Or was it more sudden?

The answer was more sudden. After the Cretaceous extinction event, three clades of frogs evolved rapidly in different parts of the world. Clades are groups that include the ancestor of a modern species and all of its descendants. The three frog clades that evolved quickly are Hyloidea, Microhylidae, and Natatanura, and they include approximately 88 percent of frogs living today.[4] Hyloidea formed in South America, while Microhylidae and Natatanura originated

TREE FROGS

There are more than 800 species of tree frogs (pictured) throughout the world.[6] However, not all of them live in trees. Some live in ponds and lakes. They have pads on the ends of their digits and long legs that help them climb. Most are lightweight so that they can walk on slim branches and leaves. The California tree frog is famous for making the "ribbit" sound heard in nature scenes in movies and TV shows.

in Africa. During this frog explosion, some frogs became arboreal. That is, they began living in and among trees, which were flourishing after the extinction event. Others began reproducing without going through a larval stage. "Frogs have been around for well over 200 million years," said David Blackburn, associate curator of amphibians and reptiles at the Florida Museum of Natural History, "but this study shows it wasn't until the extinction of the dinosaurs that we had this burst of frog diversity that resulted in the vast majority of frogs we see today."[5]

One way scientists know this finding makes sense is that it matches what happened to birds. After the Mesozoic ended, birds diversified and spread throughout the world. In the same way, the frog clades evolved quickly when most species of dinosaurs died out. Another way this finding makes sense is that frogs from the same clade can be found all over the world. This suggests that, after the Cretaceous extinction event, modern frogs followed similar evolutionary paths in far-reaching areas. "You could easily go to Central Africa, the Philippines and Ecuador and find what look like the same frogs that might have last shared a common ancestor 120 million years ago," said Blackburn. "These different lineages seem to have diversified in similar ways after the extinction."[7]

As scientists study modern frogs, they continue to learn about different ways in which frogs evolved. One example of this involves teeth. In 2011, Dr. John Wiens from the University of Arizona published a study about a tree frog from South America called *Gastrotheca guentheri*, which has teeth in both its upper and lower jaws. Other frogs have teeth in their upper jaws, but *G. guentheri* was the first frog alive today known to have teeth in its lower jaw too. What's remarkable about this find is that, while modern frogs' common ancestor also once had teeth in its lower jaw, that trait went extinct approximately 230 MYA. Like its ancestor, *G. guentheri* did not have teeth in its lower jaw. But 5 to 15 MYA, it redeveloped lower-jaw teeth.

Scientists believe that animals and other life-forms cannot regain a trait once it is lost due to evolution. This is called Dollo's law. For instance, frogs have lost their tails and most snakes have lost their limbs, but neither has regained that trait. The *G. guentheri* finding, however, contradicts the idea of Dollo's law. One theory is that *G. guentheri* already had upper teeth, so it didn't actually regain a lost trait. It just started growing teeth in a new area. Another theory is that other frog species had lost their teeth, but *G. guentheri* had not. Wiens, however, believes the trait did come back. As for the reason why, scientists are still looking for an explanation.

Another new finding about the evolution of frogs involves kneecaps. Scientists used to believe that tetrapods developed kneecaps when they evolved to the point of laying their eggs on land or when they started keeping fertilized eggs inside their bodies. However, a new finding suggests that kneecaps may have evolved much earlier, approximately 400 MYA, when tetrapods first left water.

In 2017, scientists at Argentina's Institute of Neotropical Biodiversity took tissue samples of 20 frogs. In eight of these samples, they found what looked like kneecaps made of fibrous cartilage. This cartilage makes a more flexible kneecap than the bony kneecap found

TOADS

True toads are frogs of the family Bufonidae. To put it another way, all toads are a type of frog. They have short, squat legs and no tails. Their skin is rough and warty. The African bufonids in the genus *Nectophrynoides* do not lay eggs. Instead, they give birth to miniature toads. Toads live all over the world except in Antarctica. They didn't live in Australia until 1935, when the government brought in 3,000 poisonous cane toads to control the beetle population.[8] Instead of helping with the beetles, cane toads became a pest, and now there are millions throughout Australia. The government encourages people to exterminate them.

Budgett's frog, or *Lepidobatrachus laevis*, has two fangs on the lower jaw in addition to teeth on the upper jaw.

in other animals such as humans. It allows frogs to jump and leap more easily and gives them a cushion for their joints. "The resting position in frogs is analogous to the jumping position in humans, so the knees of frogs are under constant stress, and the kneecap [made of fibrous cartilage] might alleviate this," says Virginia Abdala of Argentina's Institute.[9]

The presence of these kneecaps could be a sign that kneecaps evolved in frogs first, before other tetrapods began laying eggs on land or retaining fertilized eggs. But not all scientists believe the fibrous cartilage is a kneecap. In addition, thousands of frogs exist today, and the cartilage was found in just eight specimens.[10] More research is needed before coming to a conclusion about the evolution of kneecaps in frogs.

TODAY'S FROGS

There are more than 7,000 species of frogs living today.[11] They live everywhere on Earth except extremely cold places such as Antarctica, at very high altitudes, and on some remote ocean islands. Some frogs, however, manage to live above the desert, while others can survive at 14,960-foot (4,560 m) elevations. Some even live above the Arctic Circle. Frogs are most abundant in tropical climates, especially rain forests. For example, more than 80 species of frogs live in eastern Ecuador in the Amazon basin.[12]

AMERICAN BULLFROG

American bullfrogs are the largest frogs in North America and can grow up to eight inches (20 cm) in length.[15] They range from Canada to Mexico and live in freshwater marshes, lakes, and ponds. They are green or brown with dark-brown spots. As nocturnal animals, they eat at night by waiting for prey such as mice, birds, fish, snakes, and insects to come by. Then they lunge and grab the food in their large mouths. Male bullfrogs make a distinctive low mooing sound.

Frogs vary greatly in size and characteristics, and females are usually larger than males. One of the smallest frogs is *Paedophryne amauensis*. It measures just 0.3 inches (7.7 mm) and is smaller than a dime.[13] The largest frog is the goliath frog from West Africa at 12 inches (30 cm).[14] Most frogs have smooth, moist skin. But some frogs, such as true toads, have rough skin covered in bumps. This is most likely an adaptation for living in an arid environment.

Some members of *Rana sylvatica* live in parts of Alaska and Canada. Special adaptations help them tolerate the cold.

In one family of tree frogs, the Centrolenidae, some species have see-through skin on their undersides, making the internal organs visible. And while most frogs breathe through both their lungs and their skin, one species from Borneo, *Barbourula kalimantanensis*, only breathes through its skin. It does not have lungs.

Most frogs jump with their long, powerful hind legs. But some walk, rather than jump, along branches. They use the opposing digits on their hands and feet to grip the branches. Others burrow with short hind legs. Arboreal frogs that live in trees have sticky pads on their fingers and toes. Many have webbing between digits that aids in swimming. All frogs have poison glands, and some frogs are brilliantly colored to warn off predators. Most frogs eat insects. Larger frogs eat vertebrates including small rodents and even other frogs.

To reproduce, many species of frogs gather near fresh water during mating season. The male frog produces a mating call that is distinctive to its species. Even though most frogs are calm by nature, some males kick, bite, and bump away the competition. The South American *Boana faber* uses a sharp spine on its thumb to ward off other males. In Central America, *Oophaga pumilio* wrestles other males up in the trees until one falls to the ground.

Some frogs, such as the American bullfrog, produce as many as 20,000 eggs at a time.[16] Most frogs lay their eggs in calm fresh water and attach the eggs to sticks or rocks. *Boana faber*, however, builds muddy nests along riverbanks. Other species lay their eggs on land, and then adults carry the tadpoles on their backs to fresh water. More unusual is Darwin's frog in South America. The male of this species carries the eggs in its vocal sac until baby frogs emerge, fully formed, from its mouth. With midwife toads, the male carries the eggs around his legs until they hatch. And in the marsupial frogs in the Andes, the female carries the eggs in a pouch.

Once the eggs are laid, larvae develop inside the eggs and hatch, usually in water. The tadpoles live in the water and undergo metamorphosis. During this time, hind legs grow, first as buds and then into limbs with toes and webbing. Forelimbs, or arms, grow next through the gill coverings. The tail shrinks until it is absorbed into the body. Jaws and teeth develop, along with eyelids and mucous glands in the skin.

Some tadpoles grow into frogs in approximately two months. The spadefoot toads of North America live in small rain puddles and have to finish metamorphosis before the puddles dry up. Tree frogs deposit their eggs in water trapped in leaves high up in the trees. Some tadpoles remain in the trees as they turn into frogs, while others, such as *Dendropsophus ebraccatus* from Central America, drop into a pond below the tree and finish developing there. And some frogs, such as *Eleutherodactylus* of the Caribbean, do not go through a larval stage at all. Instead, fully formed miniature frogs emerge from eggs.

COLORATION

Some frogs are green or brown and blend in with their environments. But others, such as the dart frog, are brilliantly colored with blue, orange-red, and neon yellow. These striking colors and patterns make them stand out from vegetation and rocks. Molly Cummings of the University of Texas at Austin studied these frogs. She looked at dart frogs that lived on a series of islands 10,000 years ago in what would become modern-day Panama.[17]

What she found was that frogs developed coloration to both defend from predators and to attract mates. Cummings discovered that those with the most vivid colors—making them most visible to predators—also had the strongest poison. Those with less-lethal poison had more muted colors, which made it easier for them to hide from predators.

Cummings also looked at how birds, a top frog predator, saw color. Birds can see more colors than humans, but they cannot distinguish between levels of brightness in color. Frogs, on the other hand, can easily detect brightness. Cummings concluded that frogs developed extremely bright colors not to keep birds away. They did so to attract mates.

CHAPTER SIX

Salamanders

Salamanders, of the order Caudata, do not boast nearly as many species as frogs, but they still have a tremendous diversity of life histories, reproductive strategies, and ways of interacting with the environment. There are approximately 716 species today.[1] Most scientists believe frogs and salamanders are more closely related to each other than to any other animal. Together, they form a clade named Batrachia. This is because scientists believe frogs and salamanders evolved from the same animals and eventually split apart. An early ancestor of both frogs

The axolotl is one of the species of salamander that keeps its gills throughout its life.

and salamanders was *Gerobatrachus*, sometimes called a frogamander. It was probably a relative of the Batrachia clade. *Gerobatrachus* lived about 290 MYA and had both frog and salamander traits. It had a frog-like wide skull, but its anklebones resembled those of a salamander.

Sometime in the Permian, 299 to 252 MYA, salamanders and frogs separated and began individual evolutionary paths. The first true salamanders appeared in the middle of the Jurassic. One example of this is *Karaurus*, an ancient salamander that lived in Asia approximately 161 MYA, toward the end of the Jurassic. It measured eight inches (20 cm) in length with a heavy build and a broad, triangular skull with eyes that pointed upward.[2] It lived primarily in fresh water and ate snails, insects, and crustaceans.

Beiyanerpeton jianpingensis lived approximately 157 MYA. This salamander measured four inches (10 cm) in length.[3] With a long tail and short limbs, it probably resembled today's salamanders. Because it had gills, it lived mostly in or around the water. This fossil is the oldest example of Salamandroidea, a suborder of salamanders that includes members that are still alive today. This suborder includes more than 600 species.[4]

Scientists have found more fossils from the Mesozoic era, but these specimens did not exhibit any new or unusual traits. Many of today's salamanders descended directly from

salamanders from the Mesozoic era. Modern salamanders appeared after the extinction event at the end of the Mesozoic.

An example of one of the more recent salamanders is *Ensatina eschscholtzii*. Ten MYA, it began migrating south from the Northern California redwood forest, and it took two distinct paths. Some wandered into the forest of the Sierra Nevada. Others stayed in the mountains along the coast. Both groups avoided the Central Valley in between the two regions because the climate was too dry and hot for salamanders.

The salamanders that moved into the forest developed camouflage in order to blend into the environment and avoid predators. Over millions of years, they developed very distinct

GIANT SALAMANDER

The giant salamanders of China and Japan haven't changed much in 170 million years. They belong to the family Cryptobranchidae, which dates back to the Jurassic. The giant salamanders are the largest amphibians alive and can grow up to six feet (1.8 m) in length and weigh 110 pounds (50 kg). They live in the water and breathe through their skin. At mating time, the males find a den under rocks or in large hollows at the bottoms of streams. Females then lay 400 to 500 eggs in the dens, and the males guard the eggs from predators such as fish. The males stay there until the eggs are hatched, unless they die from injuries suffered while keeping the eggs safe. The larvae are surprisingly small at just longer than one inch (3 cm) in length.[5] As they grow into adults, they change very little besides in length and retain most larval features. Giant salamanders can live for 50 years.[6]

Some spotted
E. eschscholtzii live
in the foothills of
the Sierra Nevada
in California.

markings, such as brown with orange splotches and black with yellow splotches. The farther

south, the more distinct the markings.

The salamanders that followed the coastal mountains developed a different kind of

camouflage. Instead of trying to blend in with their environment, these salamanders took on

the red coloration and behavior of a type of poisonous newt. In this way, they stood out to

predators, but since they looked poisonous, they were protected. Both the forest salamanders

Some yellow-eyed
E. eschscholtzii
live along the coast
near San Francisco,
California.

and the coastal salamander began as one species, *E. eschscholtzii*, but are now essentially different species today.

Another type of salamander that developed more recently, about 3.4 MYA, is *Ambystoma talpoideum*, or the mole salamander. The unique feature of *A. talpoideum* is that it is unisex. That means all members of this species are one sex, and in the case of *A. talpoideum*, they are all female. They reproduce by cloning themselves and sometimes acquiring DNA from the sperm

The mole salamander lives in the southeastern United States.

of other salamanders that is left in twigs and leaves. This DNA from other species then gets integrated into their own DNA. What makes *A. talpoideum* even more unusual is that, while most unisex species last approximately 100,000 years, it has lasted millions.

In 2018, researchers at Ohio State University obtained DNA from 100 *A. talpoideum* salamanders and used new technology to study them. They theorized that the salamanders had acquired DNA from other species fairly often. However, their research showed this was not the case. "This research shows that millions of years went by where they weren't taking DNA from other species," said Rob Denton, a graduate student at Ohio State. "And then there were short bursts where they did it more frequently."[7] As for how and why *A. talpoideum* has lasted for so long as a unisex animal, scientists are still looking for answers. For this study, the researchers only looked at salamanders from one area, so *A. talpoideum* from other areas might shed new light on the data. Also, researchers want to look at unisex plants and other unisex animals to see if there are patterns in common with *A. talpoideum*.

NEWTS

Newts are a type of salamander. They live all over the world, usually around water. The red-spotted newt in the eastern United States has an unusual growing pattern. They begin their lives in water as larvae. Then they develop into a juvenile called an eft (pictured) and are colored bright orange with black spots. Efts spend several years on land while they are not yet able to breed. Then the efts go back in the water. They grow a longer tail, and their skin becomes thinner so they can breathe and swim more easily. Eventually, they emerge as adults, but now with green skin on their upper bodies and yellow underneath.

SIRENS

Sirens are a type of salamander with only two short front limbs and no hind legs. They look like eels and are colored gray, brown, or green. Sirens burrow in mud at the bottom of streams or marshes and eat insects and other invertebrates. Females lay their eggs in water or on the leaves of water plants. When baby sirens emerge, they are fully formed like adults. No larval stage is necessary. The greater siren lives mostly in the eastern United States and grows between 20 and 35 inches (50–90 cm) in length.[8]

TODAY'S SALAMANDERS

Salamanders mainly live in moist forested areas in northern temperate climates, both on land and in water. Approximately one-tenth of salamanders live in tropical regions. The Salamandridae family, which includes newts and true salamanders, lives in parts of the Himalayas, Vietnam, northern Africa, and several islands. Some ambystomatids, which include mole salamanders, live on the Mexican Plateau. Salamanders without lungs and that breathe exclusively through their skin live in tropical regions. Other salamanders live in North America, Japan, China, and western Europe.

Modern salamanders are usually four to six inches (10–15 cm) in length, though they can be as small as 1.5 inches (4 cm) and as large as

Some newts spend their entire lives in water.

six feet (1.8 m).[9] They have smooth, moist skin and glands containing both mucus and poison.

They can breathe through their skin as well as their lungs. The lungless species, however,

only breathe through their skin and the mucous membranes in their throats and mouths.

The arboreal salamanders live in the tropics. Most are gray or brown, but the more poisonous

salamanders can be more colorful.

Some salamanders
protect their eggs
while they develop.

Most salamanders are nocturnal and may stay hidden until mating season. They hide under fallen branches and rocks, within cracks in the soil, or up in trees. They tend to stay in a small area of approximately 30 to 40 square feet (3–4 sq m). It is not unusual to find up to 1,000 salamanders in one acre (0.4 ha) of land.[10] Terrestrial salamanders mainly eat insects by capturing them with their quickly moving tongues. Aquatic salamanders eat invertebrates by drawing both water and food into their mouths.

Typically, salamanders have short bodies with tails as long as their bodies. They move using their legs and by twisting their bodies from side to side. Most keep their gills throughout their lives, even after they move to land. But some lose their gills, and others never have them. Those without gills bypass the larval stage in development and hatch fully formed. Some salamanders, such as *Pseudobranchus*, spend their entire lives in water and do not have hind legs. *Proteus* salamanders are blind and live in caves. Arboreal salamanders have long legs and tails that can grasp branches and leaves.

SHOOTING TONGUE

Salamanders have an amazing ability to use their tongues to capture prey such as insects. The *Hydromantes platycephalus* from California, for instance, can launch its tongue at a distance 80 percent the length of its body. And it can do this in 20 thousandths of a second.[11] Scientists believe salamanders can store up energy in their tongues, similar to a coiled spring or a bow and arrow, and then they release their tongues in a burst of energy.

Most salamanders breed near bodies of water such as swamps, ponds, and streams, but some species breed on land and lay eggs under fallen logs or in trees. Terrestrial salamanders lay approximately five or six eggs at a time, while aquatic salamanders can deposit 400 eggs in the water.[12] Females usually stay with their eggs until hatching. During metamorphosis, salamanders lose their gills and develop a tongue pad. Their eyes and mouths get bigger, they grow eyelids, and their skulls and skin change. The larval stage can last a few days or a few years, depending on the species.

Some salamanders do not have a larval stage. These are salamanders that are fully land based. They lay their eggs on land, and the hatchling emerges as a tiny adult.

Sometimes baby salamanders are visible inside their eggs.

Caecilians can be mistaken for worms and snakes.

CHAPTER SEVEN

Caecilians

Caecilians are the least understood of the three amphibian orders and have the fewest species. Unlike frogs and salamanders, they have no limbs and are usually blind, resembling large earthworms. Today, there are slightly more than 200 known species of caecilians.[1]

CAECILIAN EVOLUTION

Scientists used to believe caecilians separated from frogs and salamanders during the Permian. However, in 2017, scientists from the Keck School of Medicine of the University of Southern California released a study about caecilian evolution. It showed that caecilians separated from frogs and salamanders during the Carboniferous. This was much earlier than previously thought.

The scientists had originally found the fossils used in their study in the 1990s. But it wasn't until 2017 that they had their breakthrough. This was because new technology allowed them to learn more about the animal. Using 3-D X-rays, they reassembled parts of a skull, a spinal column, ribs, a shoulder, and legs. What they found was that this fossil, *Chinlestegophis jenkinsi*, was the oldest ancestor of caecilians ever found. *Chinlestegophis jenkinsi* was also part of a group of amphibians called stereospondyls that lived during the Triassic.

Chinlestegophis jenkinsi had been found in a two-inch- (5 cm) wide burrow. Its skull was less than one inch (2.5 cm) in length, and although its body length was unknown, scientists thought the animal resembled a small salamander. It had four limbs, unlike today's limbless caecilians, suggesting that caecilians lost their limbs over time.[2] It also had small eyes that worked, unlike many caecilians today that have eyes that do not help them see much. It also had characteristics such as smaller eye sockets that indicated it was a burrowing animal. So it most likely lived underground, probably because the summers

STEREOSPONDYLS

Stereospondyls are a type of temnospondyl that lived in the Triassic period. They were known for their toilet seat–shaped heads. And like other temnospondyls, they resembled large crocodiles. One type was Capitosauria. It lived in rivers, lakes, and deltas across the supercontinent of Pangaea. Some reached 20 feet (6 m) in length.[3] They probably lived on the bottom of a body of water and lunged at prey that swam close by.

Some caecilians'
eyes are hidden
under bone.

during the Triassic in its habitat, what is now Colorado, would have been very hot. It dug down to the water table and stayed there, eating insects for food.

This fossil changed how scientists believed caecilians evolved. Scientists previously thought that caecilians could not have descended from stereospondyls because scientists believed that stereospondyls had died out before caecilians. But after studying *C. jenkinsi*, some scientists now believe caecilians did descend from stereospondyls, though others disagree.

Because of caecilians' small size and underground existence, the fossil record has few examples of them. Besides *C. jenkinsi*, another significant caecilian fossil is *Eocaecilia*. It is from approximately 199 MYA in the early part of the Jurassic and was found in Arizona. Measuring six inches (15 cm) in length, it had small limbs that looked like they may have once been longer.[4] This showed caecilians evolving away from limbs entirely, which meant *Eocaecilia* closely resembled today's caecilians. Beyond these examples, only a scattering of caecilians from more recent time periods have been found.

TODAY'S CAECILIANS

Caecilians live in the Americas, Asia, Africa, the Philippines, Sri Lanka (an island off the coast of India), the Amazon rain forest and the Seychelles (islands off eastern Africa). They thrive in

An artist showed *Eocaecilia*'s small limbs, which could indicate that caecilians gradually lost their limbs.

humid tropical regions near streams and rivers where they can hide in loose leaves and soil. The smallest caecilians are *Idiocranium russeli* in West Africa and *Grandisonia brevis* in the Seychelles. Both measure approximately four inches (10 cm) in length. The largest caecilian is *Caecilia thompsoni* in the Americas at about five feet (1.5 m) in length.[5]

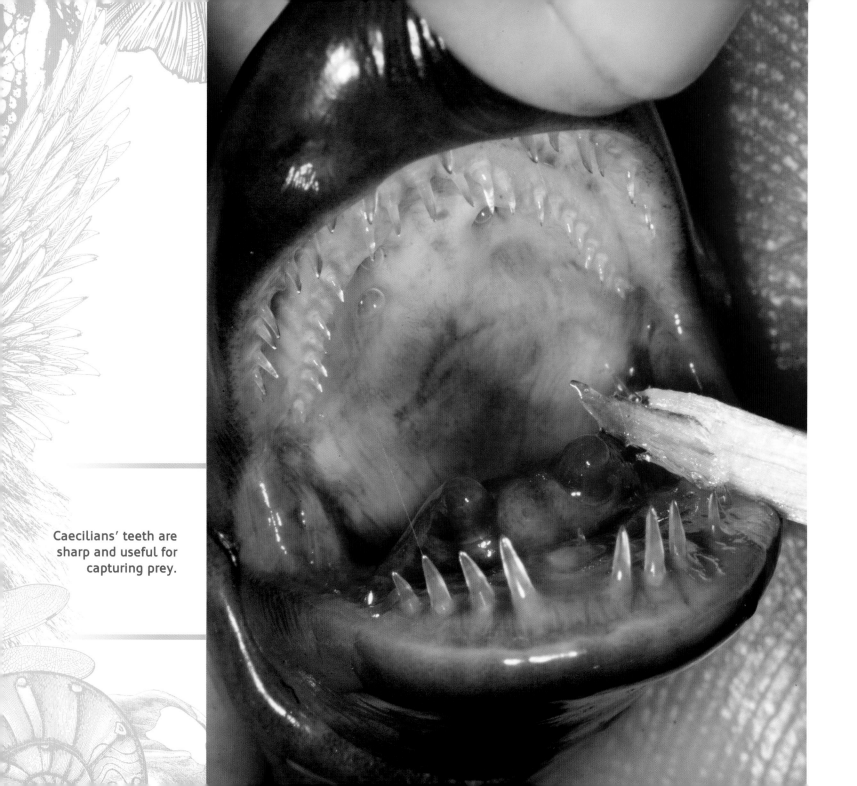

Caecilians' teeth are sharp and useful for capturing prey.

Caecilians are black, orange, gray, brown, or yellow. They have long bodies and short tails, with between 95 and 285 vertebrae in their trunks.[6] Their heads are blunt and pointy, and their skin is shiny and covered with growth rings called annuli that go around their bodies. These annuli can be used to estimate how old the caecilian is. The skin has glands filled with poison to protect them from predators. Caecilians can't hear, so they rely on vibrations in the ground to provide information about food or predators. They also use tentacles that sit between their eyes and nostrils. The tentacles help them sense their environments. Most caecilians are blind. In fact, the name *caecilian* comes from the Latin word *caecus*, which means "sightless."

RINGED CAECILIAN

The ringed caecilian of eastern South America lives in the tropics. It pushes through soil with its head, using it like a pointy shovel to clear the way. The scaly rings along its body help it wriggle forward. It raises its body off the ground and pushes off with the part still touching the ground. Movement comes in waves. And as it moves, it uses its tentacles to sense prey and chemicals in the soil.

PROTRUDING EYES

Some caecilians have no eyes. Some have eyes located within an eye socket but covered with skin, and others have eyes hidden under bone. Then there are the scolecomorphids. Members of this family of caecilians from Africa have unique eyes that move out of the head. A tentacle opening is close to the eyes and along the tip of the snout. When the tentacle is resting, the eye stays under the skull. But when the tentacle extends all the way out, the eye pops out of the skull and travels down the tentacle. A portion of the tentacle allows light to enter the eye so the caecilian can see.

Caecilians usually burrow underground, using their pointy heads to help dig tunnels. They have dozens of sharp teeth and eat earthworms, termites, small snakes, lizards, frogs, and other caecilians. They swallow their food whole. Other species live aboveground or in the water. Aquatic species eat fish, eels, and invertebrates.

Some caecilians breed year-round, while others, including *Ichthyophis glutinosus* from Sri Lanka, only mate during the rainy season. Depending on the species, caecilians either lay eggs or produce their young fully formed without eggs. Most lay eggs in burrows close to a body of water, up to 50 eggs at a time.[7] After hatching, the larvae live in the water and eat plankton. Metamorphosis consists of growing one lung, developing annuli, thickening their skin, and growing tentacles. After metamorphosis, young caecilians leave the water and move onto land, where they can burrow into the earth. However, *Siphonops annulatus* from the Brazilian rain forest doesn't go through metamorphosis. After laying its eggs, the female forms a coil around them until they hatch, fully formed. The young caecilians remain close to the mother's body and feed off the mucus on her skin that is rich in proteins.

BOULENGER'S CAECILIAN

Boulenger's caecilian lives in Tanzania in southeastern Africa. It hides out in the loose earth of tropical forests. Like many other caecilians, it waits for prey to pass nearby. Then it uses its powerful jaws to grab its food. Two rows of teeth, curved backward, help it hang on to its prey, and strong muscles in its mouth help its jaws close. Boulenger's caecilians eat prey such as termites.

CHAPTER EIGHT

Studying Amphibians Today

Current knowledge about the evolution of amphibians changes all the time. Scientists are always looking for new fossils all over the world, and researchers are applying new technology to the study of amphibians. Modern amphibians are also being studied, which can lead to a greater understanding of evolution.

NEW TECHNOLOGY

One way scientists will be able to learn more about amphibian evolution is through the use of new technology, both on ancient fossils and modern species. With CT scans, scientists can scan fossils while they are still in the surrounding rock. Chipping away at a fossil so it can be studied

CT scans can help scientists learn about amphibian fossils and amphibians alive today.

by the naked eye can take years of meticulous work, but creating a virtual image of the bones inside the rock can speed up the process immensely.

Scientists use CT scans to create 3-D models on a computer. Then they animate parts of the fossil so they can see how the animal might have moved or walked. With virtual 3-D models, scientists can also replace missing bones or fix skulls that may have been flattened. They can add soft tissue, such as muscles or the brain. And they can make the information easily available to other scientists.

In 2012, Stephanie Pierce—from the Royal Veterinary College at the time—wanted to see how *Ichthyostega* could walk on land. To the naked eye, the fossil looked like a modern amphibian. But could it move like one? She found the best-preserved fossils from the 300 specimens in existence and put them in a CT scanner.[1] CT scanners take hundreds of X-rays

CT SCANS

Paleontologists use CT scanners that are slightly different from the ones in hospitals. In order to penetrate rocks, they use stronger X-rays that would be harmful to living organisms. When a CT scan is performed, the specimen is placed in the scanner. Then hundreds of X-rays are taken while the fossil is rotated to get every possible angle. The scans are uploaded into software that puts all the pieces together into a 3-D image.

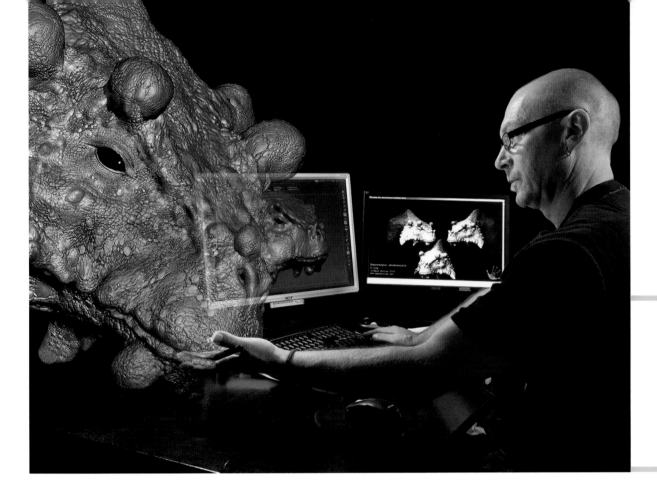

CT scans allow scientists to create models of fossils. They also allow scientists to rebuild what extinct species might have looked like.

from all angles. It took her two years, but eventually, she was able to make a 3-D virtual model of an *Ichthyostega* skeleton.

"It makes *Ichthyostega* a bit more tangible," said Pierce. "It's not just a fossil laying in a rock now. It's an animal that's coming to life." The model was animated and put online for anyone to see. It showed how the shoulders and hips could move up and down and side to side. But they

SCANNING VERTEBRATES

Blackburn and Summers thought it would be a good idea to scan all vertebrates, not just fish and frogs. They contacted the National Science Foundation and obtained a $2.5 million grant to do so. Sixteen museums and universities became involved in the project, which was scheduled to last four years and scan more than 20,000 specimens. Of these, 1,000 would be soaked in iodine to better see the brain, heart, muscles, and other internal parts. Many 3-D images are available to teachers, scientists, students, and the public on the MorphoSource website.[3] Since 2014, several other places have been storing information on fossils, such as DigiMorph at the University of Texas at Austin, Morphbank at Florida State University, and Morphobank at Stony Brook University in New York.

couldn't rotate. This meant *Ichthyostega* couldn't have walked on land like a modern salamander, as many scientists had thought. *Ichthyostega* would not have been able to support its weight or put its feet flat on the ground. So while it walked on land, it didn't walk very well. The technology brought new insights to a fossil that had been around for more than 50 years.[2]

In 2016, Adam Summers, a professor from the University of Washington, was continuing his work of CT scanning fish that were preserved in liquid. From his scans, he made 3-D representations of the fish and posted the images online. He also tweeted about them on Twitter, using the hashtag #ScanAllFishes. Meanwhile, other scientists were busy doing the same with amphibians, including many frogs.

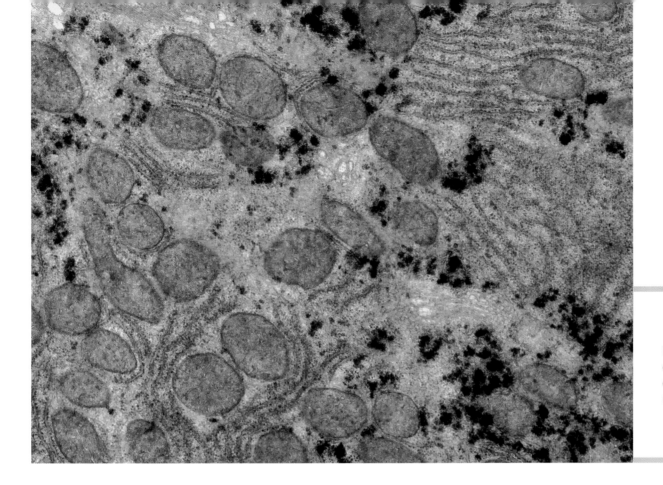

Electron microscopy can be used to see detail down to the microscopic level.

A group of museums proposed a project called oVert, which stands for "Open Exploration of Vertebrate Diversity in 3D." David Blackburn, a herpetologist from the Florida Museum of Natural History, saw Summers's Twitter #ScanAllFishes project. He invited Summers to join oVert.

Another technology researchers take advantage of is electron microscopy. This uses beams of electrons to create images. For instance, this technology allowed scientists in Germany to see the type of pollen inside a bird's stomach without removing the bird from the rock. Based on the pollen, they were able to date the bird at 47 million years old. It was the oldest bird fossil ever found.

Particle accelerators are also used to study fossils. They produce beams of charged particles, such as protons or electrons, to create bright and precise X-rays. Features smaller than 1/100 the thickness of human hair can be seen with this method.[4]

EXISTING AMPHIBIANS

One limitation paleontologists are discovering is that they do not have enough information on today's amphibians. How modern animals compare to their ancient ancestors is important to understanding evolution. For instance, Mark Norell, chair of paleontology at the American Museum of Natural History, wanted to reconstruct dinosaur brains. To do so, he needed to compare dinosaur brains with brains of modern birds. He found, however, that there was very little information available on birds. So he and his fellow scientists took matters into their own hands. They built a helmet that can go on a bird's head and allows the birds to be scanned. "Previously, most paleontologists were primarily trained as geologists," Norell says. "Now . . . most of us consider ourselves to be biologists who work on fossils sometimes."[5]

In 2018, two scientists published a paper about existing amphibians in the scientific journal *Nature Ecology & Evolution*. The topic of the paper was the amphibian family tree, or its phylogeny. Walter Jetz, associate professor of ecology and evolutionary biology at Yale University, and R. Alexander Pyron, from George Washington University, had mapped the generations of almost all amphibian species alive today.

Jetz and Pyron looked for patterns in amphibians, how they changed over time, and how certain species became isolated from other species. They wanted to see how different species

Amphibians provide valuable services to their ecosystems, including controlling insect populations.

evolved in unique ways. And what they discovered was that some species carried traits with more than 100 million years of evolutionary history. And others had developed specific traits in response to their ecosystems. "A worldwide focus on all species allows us to link threats and evolutionary history across regions in a way that was not possible previously," Pyron said.[6]

It is important to study amphibians to see their unique place in the evolutionary family tree. But it is also important because amphibian evolution can tell us about the ways environments

have changed. The US Geological Survey is monitoring amphibian populations with its Amphibian Research and Monitoring Initiative (ARMI). It is taking note of declining amphibian populations to see how amphibians are responding to changes in the environment. It is also researching reasons for the falling amphibian populations and studying possible solutions to stop and hopefully reverse these declines. "Amphibians do a lot of the important jobs," says a USGS statement on the survey study. "They control pests, provide medicines, feed other animals, and help make ecosystems work. They are extraordinary, diverse, beautiful animals. They have social value that inspires art and culture, and they are an ancient source of biodiversity."[7]

FIGHTING A FUNGUS

Some animals evolve in response to life-threatening fungi. A deadly chytrid fungus has ravaged frog populations around the world. Called *Batrachochytrium dendrobatidis*, it grows on frogs' skin and stops them from getting water and air through their skin. Already, the chytrid fungus has caused some species to become extinct. But in Panama, the frog population is making a comeback. Scientists studied the fungus to find out why. They compared it to a sample from 2004 and found that the fungus did not change very much. Scientists then studied the frogs. They compared frogs from today to the descendants of frogs from the area before the fungus infestation. Today's frogs have a stronger immune system. They are evolving in response to a change in their environment.

ESSENTIAL FACTS

			Ichthyostega Acanthostega	Pederpes	Gerobatrachus	
541–485.4 million years ago (MYA)	485.4–443.8 MYA	443.8–419.2 MYA	419.2–358.9 MYA	358.9–298.9 MYA	298.9–251.9 MYA	
CAMBRIAN	ORDOVICIAN	SILURIAN	DEVONIAN	CARBONIFEROUS	PERMIAN	

NUMBER OF SPECIES

There are more than 6,970 species of frogs, approximately 716 species of salamander, and slightly more than 200 species of caecilians.

IMPORTANT ANIMALS AND SPECIMENS

- *Ichthyostega* lived 370–360 MYA. This tetrapod may have been the first animal to set foot on land.

- *Acanthostega* lived 370–360 MYA. This tetrapod showed that limbs developed in the water and not on land as previously thought.

- *Pederpes* was a lobe-finned fish from 350 MYA. Most scientists believe it was the first tetrapod to live on land.

- *Gerobatrachus* lived 290 MYA and was a relative of modern amphibians. With both frog and salamander traits, it was called a frogamander.

- *Chinlestegophis jenkinsi* lived during the Triassic. This is the oldest ancestor of caecilians ever found.

- *Triadobatrachus massinoti* lived 250 MYA. It had both ancient and modern frog traits.

- *Eocaecilia* lived approximately 199 MYA. Its small limbs show how caecilians became limbless.

Chinlestegophis jenkinsi *Triadobatrachus massinoti*	*Eocaecilia*				
251.9–201.3 MYA	201.3–145 MYA	145–66 MYA	66–23 MYA	23–2.6 MYA	2.6 MYA–present
TRIASSIC	JURASSIC	CRETACEOUS	PALEOGENE	NEOGENE	QUATERNARY

IMPORTANT SCIENTISTS

- Gunnar Säve-Söderbergh discovered *Ichthyostega* in Greenland in 1931.

- Jennifer Clack discovered that early tetrapods developed the ability to walk in the water.

- Jean Piveteau determined that *T. massinoti* had both ancient and modern frog traits.

QUOTE

"Frogs have been around for well over 200 million years, but . . . it wasn't until the extinction of the dinosaurs that we had this burst of frog diversity that resulted in the vast majority of frogs we see today."

—David Blackburn, associate curator of amphibians and reptiles at the Florida Museum of Natural History

GLOSSARY

amniote
An animal whose embryo develops in a thin membrane called an amnion.

arboreal
Living in trees.

clade
A group of species that all descended from a common ancestor.

CT scan
A collection of two-dimensional X-ray images that can be used to create a three-dimensional image of a body part or fossil.

DNA
Deoxyribonucleic acid, the chemical that is the basis of genetics, through which various traits are passed from parent to child.

electron
A particle in an atom that holds a negative charge of electricity.

fossil record
The history of life as known from studying fossils.

gene
A unit of hereditary information found in a chromosome.

invertebrate
An animal without a spinal column.

larva
An immature form of an animal that changes its body form through metamorphosis.

metamorphosis
A change or transformation, such as when tadpoles change into frogs.

mucous membrane
A thin layer containing glands that produce mucus, a slippery substance that covers the skin of amphibians.

paleontology
The study of past life, involving fossils and previous geological periods.

phylogeny
The evolutionary history of a species or group of organisms.

species
A group of organisms that are very similar and can breed with each other.

supercontinent
A large continent from which other continents broke away.

terrestrial
Of or relating to the land.

tetrapod
An animal that evolved from an ancestor that had two sets of limbs; amphibians, mammals, and reptiles are all tetrapods.

vertebrae
Segments in the spinal column made of bone or cartilage.

vertebrate
An animal with a spinal column and a brain that is part of its nervous system.

SELECTED BIBLIOGRAPHY

Parker, Steve, ed. *Evolution: The Whole Story*. Firefly, 2015.

Van Hoose, Natalie. "Extinction Event That Wiped Out Dinosaurs Cleared Way for Frogs." *Florida Museum of Natural History*, 3 July 2017, floridamuseum.ufl.edu. Accessed 24 July 2018.

Zimmer, Carl. "In the Beginning Was the Mudskipper?" *Discover*, 23 May 2012, blogs.discovermagazine.com. Accessed 24 July 2018.

Zug, George R., and William E. Duellman. "Amphibian." *Encyclopædia Britannica*, 19 Aug. 2016, britannica.com. Accessed 24 July 2018.

FURTHER READINGS

Howell, Catherine Herbert. *National Geographic Pocket Guide to Reptiles and Amphibians of North America*. National Geographic, 2015.

Perdew, Laura. *Bringing Back Our Wetlands*. Abdo, 2018.

Schutten, Jan Paul. *The Mystery of Life: How Nothing Became Everything*. Aladdin, 2015.

ONLINE RESOURCES

To learn more about the evolution of amphibians, visit **abdobooklinks.com**. These links are routinely monitored and updated to provide the most current information available.

MORE INFORMATION

For more information on this subject, contact or visit the following organizations:

AMERICAN MUSEUM OF NATURAL HISTORY
Central Park West at Seventy-Ninth St.
New York, NY 10024-5192
212-769-5100
amnh.org

One of the world's preeminent scientific and cultural museums, the American Museum of Natural History has information on paleontology, fossils, and amphibians.

SMITHSONIAN NATIONAL MUSEUM OF NATURAL HISTORY
Tenth St. and Constitution Ave. NW
Washington, DC 20560
naturalhistory.si.edu

This museum strives to understand the natural world. The Division of Amphibians and Reptiles has one of the largest collections of preserved specimens in the world.

SOURCE NOTES

CHAPTER 1. OUT OF THE WATER

1. "Ichthyostega." *Encyclopædia Britannica*, 14 Jan. 2007, britannica.com. Accessed 6 Sept. 2018.

2. Michael R. House. "Devonian Period." *Encyclopædia Britannica*, 17 July 2014, britannica.com. Accessed 6 Sept. 2018.

3. "Amphibian Species Lists." *AmphibiaWeb*, 6 Sept. 2018, amphibiaweb.org. Accessed 6 Sept. 2018.

4. "Golden Poison Frog." *National Geographic*, n.d., nationalgeographic.com. Accessed 6 Sept. 2018.

5. "Darwin's Diary." *Evolution*, n.d., pbs.org. Accessed 6 Sept. 2018.

6. "Why Do Most Species Have Five Digits on Their Hands and Feet?" *Scientific American*, 25 Apr. 2005, scientificamerican.com. Accessed 6 Sept. 2018.

CHAPTER 2. BECOMING TETRAPODS

1. R. Jamil Jonna. "Actinopterygii: Ray-Finned Fishes." *Animal Diversity Web*, 2004, animaldiversity.org. Accessed 6 Sept. 2018.

2. William E. Duellman and George R. Zug. "Amphibian." *Encyclopædia Britannica*, 19 Aug. 2016, britannica.com. Accessed 6 Sept. 2018.

3. Kevin Padian. "Tiktaalik Roseae." *Encyclopædia Britannica*, 15 January 2014, britannica.com. Accessed 6 Sept. 2018.

4. "Ichthyostega." *Encyclopædia Britannica*, 14 Jan. 2007, britannica.com. Accessed 6 Sept. 2018.

5. Carl Zimmer. "In the Beginning Was the Mudskipper?" *Discover*, 23 May 2012, blogs.discovermagazine.com. Accessed 6 Sept. 2018.

6. Helen Lewis. "The Trouble with Fossils." *New Statesman*, 2 May 2012, newstatesman.com. Accessed 6 Sept. 2018.

7. Douglas Palmer. *Evolution: The Story of Life*. University of California Press, 2009. 82.

8. Richard Cowen. *History of Life*. Wiley-Blackwell, 2013. *Google Books*, books.google.com. Accessed 6 Sept. 2018.

9. "Devonian Period." *National Geographic*, n.d., nationalgeographic.com. Accessed 6 Sept. 2018.

10. "Devonian Period."

CHAPTER 3. ANCIENT AMPHIBIANS

1. "Carboniferous Period," *National Geographic*, n.d., nationalgeographic.com. Accessed 6 Sept. 2018.

2. William E. Duellman and George R. Zug. "Amphibian." *Encyclopædia Britannica*, 19 Aug. 2016, britannica.com. Accessed 6 Sept. 2018.

3. Duellman and Zug, "Amphibian."

4. Bob Strauss. "300 Million Years of Amphibian Evolution." *ThoughtCo*, 2 July 2018, thoughtco.com. Accessed 6 Sept. 2018.

5. Steve Parker, ed. *Evolution: The Whole Story*. Firefly Books, 2015. 214–219.

6. Christine Dell'Amore. "'FedEx' Fossil Amphibian Found in Pittsburgh." *National Geographic News*, 17 Mar. 2010, news.nationalgeographic.com. Accessed 6 Sept. 2018.

7. Rainer R. Schoch. *Amphibian Evolution: The Life of Early Land Vertebrates*. Blackwell, 2014. 41.

8. Schoch, *Amphibian Evolution*, 43.

9. David Templeton. "Rare Fossil Find." *Blade*, 22 Mar. 2010, toledoblade.com. Accessed 6 Sept. 2018.

10. Parker, *Evolution*, 218–219.

11. "Carboniferous Period."

12. "Carboniferous Period."

13. "Permian Period." *National Geographic*, n.d., nationalgeographic.com. Accessed 6 Sept. 2018.

CHAPTER 4. EARLY FROGS

1. Steve Parker, ed. *Evolution: The Whole Story*. Firefly Books, 2015. 220–223.

2. Parker, *Evolution*, 220.

3. Parker, *Evolution*, 222.

4. Barbara S. Moffet. "Unearthing the Story of Madagascar, Fossil by Fossil." *National Geographic*, 17 May 2011, blog.nationalgeographic.org. Accessed 6 Sept. 2018.

5. Bob Strauss. "Prehistoric Amphibian Pictures and Profiles." *ThoughtCo*, 17 Mar. 2017, thoughtco.com. Accessed 6 Sept. 2018.

6. "Devil Frog." *National Geographic*, n.d., nationalgeographic.com. Accessed 6 Sept. 2018.

7. "K-T Event." *NASA*, n.d., jpl.nasa.gov. Accessed 6 Sept. 2018.

8. Roff Smith. "Here's What Happened the Day the Dinosaurs Died." *National Geographic News*, 11 June 2016, news.nationalgeographic.com. Accessed 6 Sept. 2018.

CHAPTER 5. MODERN FROGS

1. "K-T Event." *NASA*, n.d., jpl.nasa.gov. Accessed 6 Sept. 2018.

2. Natalie van Hoose. "Extinction Event That Wiped Out Dinosaurs Cleared Way for Frogs," *Florida Museum of Natural History*, 3 July 2017, floridamuseum.ufl.edu. Accessed 6 Sept. 2018.

3. Van Hoose, "Extinction Event That Wiped Out Dinosaurs."

4. Van Hoose, "Extinction Event That Wiped Out Dinosaurs."

5. Van Hoose, "Extinction Event That Wiped Out Dinosaurs."

6. "Tree Frogs." *National Wildlife Federation*, n.d., nwf.org. Accessed 6 Sept. 2018.

7. Van Hoose, "Extinction Event That Wiped Out Dinosaurs."

8. "Cane Toad." *National Geographic*, n.d., nationalgeographic.com. Accessed 6 Sept. 2018.

9. Andy Coghlan. "Frogs May Have Evolved the First Kneecaps on Earth." *New Scientist*, 7 July 2017, newscientist.com. Accessed 6 Sept. 2018.

10. Coghlan, "Frogs May Have Evolved the First Kneecaps on Earth."

11. "Amphibian Species Lists." *AmphibiaWeb*, 6 Sept. 2018, amphibiaweb.org. Accessed 6 Sept. 2018.

12. George R. Zug and William E. Duellman. "Anura." *Encyclopædia Britannica*, 17 May 2016, britannica.com. Accessed 6 Sept. 2018.

SOURCE NOTES CONTINUED

13. Christine Dell'Amore. "World's Smallest Frog Found—Fly-Size Beast Is Tiniest Vertebrate." *National Geographic News*, 13 Jan. 2012, news.nationalgeographic.com. Accessed 6 Sept. 2018.

14. Zug and Duellman, "Anura."

15. "American Bullfrog," *National Geographic*, n.d., nationalgeographic.com. Accessed 6 Sept. 2018.

16. "American Bullfrog."

17. Amy Maxmen. "How Do Tropical Frogs Get Their Stunning Colors?" *Smithsonian*, 31 Aug. 2013, smithsonianmag.com. Accessed 6 Sept. 2018.

CHAPTER 6. SALAMANDERS

1. "Species by the Numbers." *AmphibiaWeb*, 6 Sept. 2018, amphibiaweb.org. Accessed 6 Sept. 2018.

2. Rainer R. Schoch. *Amphibian Evolution: The Life of Early Land Vertebrates*. Wiley-Blackwell, 2014. *Google Books*, books.google.com. Accessed 6 Sept. 2018.

3. Jennifer Welsh. "New Jurassic Salamander Is World's Oldest." *Live Science*, 12 Mar. 2012, livescience.com. Accessed 6 Sept. 2018.

4. "Amphibian Species Lists." *AmphibiaWeb*, 6 Sept. 2018, amphibiaweb.org. Accessed 6 Sept. 2018.

5. Max Sparreboom and Yunke Wu. *"Andrias davidianus Chinese Giant Salamander: Evolution."* *Encyclopedia of Life*, 15 Oct. 2011, eol.org. Accessed 6 Sept. 2018.

6. Jason Bittel. "This Giant Salamander Isn't 200 Years Old, But It's Still Super Rare." *National Geographic News*, 16 Sept. 2015, news.nationalgeographic.com. Accessed 6 Sept. 2018.

7. "Unisexual Salamander Evolution: A Long, Strange Trip." *Phys.org*, 25 July 2018, phys.org. Accessed 6 Sept. 2018.

8. "Siren." *Encyclopædia Britannica*, 24 Aug. 2012, britannica.com. Accessed 6 Sept. 2018.

9. David B. Wake. "Caudata." *Encyclopædia Britannica*, 15 May 2014, britannica.com. Accessed 6 Sept. 2018.

10. Wake, "Caudata."

11. Victoria Gill. "Salamander's Elastic Tongue Powered by a 'Coiled Spring.'" *BBC*, 11 Oct. 2011, bbc.co.uk. Accessed 6 Sept. 2018.

12. Wake, "Caudata."

CHAPTER 7. CAECILIANS

1. "Amphibian Species Lists." *AmphibiaWeb*, 6 Sept. 2018, amphibiaweb.org. Accessed 6 Sept. 2018.

2. Zen Vuong. "Tiny Fossils Reveal Backstory of the Most Mysterious Amphibian Alive Today." *USC News*, 19 June 2017, news.usc.edu. Accessed 6 Sept. 2018.

3. Rainer R. Schoch. *Amphibian Evolution: The Life of Early Land Vertebrates*. Blackwell, 2014. 57.

4. Andrew Farke. "Scintillating Caecilian Fossils Spill New Secrets." *PLOS Blogs*, 7 Dec. 2012, blogs.plos.org. Accessed 6 Sept. 2018.

5. William E. Duellman. "Gymnophiona." *Encyclopædia Britannica*, 20 Feb. 2015, britannica.com. Accessed 6 Sept. 2018.

6. Duellman, "Gymnophiona."

7. Laurie J. Vitt and Janalee P. Caldwell. *Herpetology: An Introductory Biology of Amphibians and Reptiles*. Elsevier, 2014. *Google Books*, books.google.com. Accessed 6 Sept. 2018.

CHAPTER 8. STUDYING AMPHIBIANS TODAY

1. Ed Yong. "Virtual Resurrection Shows That Early Four-Legged Animal Couldn't Walk Very Well." *Discover*, 23 May 2012, blogs.discovermagazine.com. Accessed 6 Sept. 2018.

2. Yong, "Virtual Resurrection."

3. Ryan Cross. "New 3D Scanning Campaign Will Reveal 20,000 Animals in Stunning Detail." *Science*, 24 Aug. 2017, sciencemag.org. Accessed 6 Sept. 2018.

4. Matt Safford. "How New Tech for Ancient Fossils Could Change the Way We Understand Animals." *Smithsonian*, 5 June 2014, smithsonianmag.com. Accessed 6 Sept. 2018.

5. Safford, "How New Tech for Ancient Fossils Could Change."

6. Jim Shelton. "Human Threats to the Amphibian Tree of Life." *Phys.org*, 27 Mar. 2018, phys.org. Accessed 6 Sept. 2018.

7. Dan Vergano. "Amphibians Dying Off at Alarming Rate." *USA Today*, 22 May 2013, usatoday.com. Accessed 6 Sept. 2018.

ABOUT THE AUTHOR

Andrea Pelleschi has been writing and editing children's books for over 15 years, including novels, storybooks, novelty books, graphic novels, and educational nonfiction books. She has a master of fine arts in creative writing from Emerson College. She currently lives in Cincinnati, Ohio.